Love and Respect

Understanding Love and Mastering the Art of Loving

Dennis E. Bradford, Ph.D.

Publisher's Notes

ISBN 978-1-940487-07-6

" . . . he who understands also loves . . ."

Paracelsus

By the Same Author

The Concept of Existence
The Fundamental Ideas
A Thinker's Guide to Living Well
Mastery in 7 Steps
How to Survive College Emotionally
A Dark Time
Personal Transformation
*The Three Things the Rest of Us Should Know about Zen
        Training*
The Meditative Approach to Philosophy
How to Eat Less – Easily!
Compulsive Overeating Help
How to Stop Emotional Eating
How to Become Happily Published
Belly Fat Blast with Anna Wright
Getting Things Done
Weight Lifting
Emotional Eating
12 Publicity Mistakes that Keep Marketers Poor
It's Not Just About the Money!
40 Top Marketing Mistakes

Contents

1: What's the Problem?

What's the problem about understanding and practicing love? It's impossible to clarify the answer without first clarifying the question.

The word 'love' is so ubiquitous that some thinkers refuse to use it. Supposedly, we love our mothers and our friends, but we also love chocolate cake and fried chicken. We may love fishing or having sex. We may love warm, sunny days or the thunder and lightning of storms. We may think of love as the process of loving or we may think of it as an object or an emotion or a desire. We may think that we love love!

Many people seem to approach the topic of love with the assumption that one of our most fundamental needs or wants as human beings is to be loved. The word 'love' is used so frequently in so many diverse ways that it's simply unclear what its nature is supposed to be. Many seem to think that the word 'love' is a noun that denotes an object to be gained.

If we are to make any progress whatsoever understanding the nature and practice of love, there's no choice but to regiment ordinary language in a specific way. This involves no criticism of how most people normally think or talk; in other words, I'm not claiming that it's wrong to use 'love' in other ways. It's simply a tactic that attempts to prevent misunderstanding.

In general, does the noun or the verb come first? Think back to when you were learning to read. Did you learn to read and use 'Spot runs' before or after learning 'Spot is a runner'? The verb came first, didn't it? If Spot runs, then automatically Spot is a runner. '(To) run' is the infinitive of the verb, whereas 'runner' is a noun.

It's possible to see that Spot is running, but, except for seeing Spot running, is it possible to see that Spot is a runner? Have you ever seen a runner in abstraction from something running? It seems that nouns come from verbs and are more abstract than verbs.

Whether that's true or not, it's good enough to distinguish the noun 'love' from the verb '(to) love.' Because nouns are more abstract and verbs are more concrete, let's agree to approach the nature of love by thinking of it as an activity rather than as a noun. After all, for example, although we frequently observe loving acts, there's no such thing as observing love itself (in abstraction from, in the case of humans, human actions).

Our topic, then, is human loving. Approaching it as an activity is immediately helpful. Why?

We all know that, with the exception of simple natural activities such as breathing, mastering activities requires skills. It's impossible to brew a good cup of coffee or write a novel or play basketball or read a book well without doing something that requires learning. These are all relatively complicated activities that require ability, understanding, effort, and skill to master—and we usually spend our waking hours engaged in such activities.

In the case of an important, complex activity like loving, it's important to approach it as if it's an activity to be mastered rather than just a thing or object to be gained or possessed. We all have the ability to be loving. Being loving is doing something; it's an activity at which we are able to become better.

If so, this gives us a way forward, a coherent plan. *First*, what is love? *Second*, how do we master the practice of loving?

This book provides my answers to those questions.

I offer reasons in favor of my answers. Once you understand them, examine and evaluate those reasons for yourself. If they are similar to your own, you may put this book down having become more confident about your own answers. If they are dissimilar to your own, then either you'll find my reasons persuasive or you won't. If you re-main unpersuaded, then you'll think that your reasons will have withstood attack and have more confidence in them. If, though, you are persuaded by my reasons, you may simply let your old answers go and adopt better ones.

So the process of examining human loving is one that cannot but benefit you.

Notice that 'human' is a critical part of the phrase 'human loving.' It's an obvious logical point that we have insufficiently targeted our subject matter unless we clarify the meaning of 'human.' As Erich Fromm correctly states: "Any theory of love must begin with a theory of . . . human existence." Incidentally, this is true of many other views including views about politics, religion, and economics; they all must be grounded on an account of human being.

If we make a mistake about what it is to be a human being, we have no chance of understanding human loving (or politics or religion or economics and so on). So let's tackle the question of what it is to be a human being.

2: Being Human

The best way to begin to understand the nature of being human is to examine yourself rather than start with one of the many theories of human nature. Our goal is to understand loving and to become better lovers. By way of contrast, it is not necessary even to attempt to answer all the possible questions about the nature of being human.

It's not enough just to be skeptical of the views of others; since we ourselves may have been insufficiently skeptical in the past, it's important also to be skeptical of our own views, particularly of those views to which we have become fondly attached. However uncomfortable, it's important not to build into our account our own favorite biases.

A sufficient reason for doing this is so that we may become more skillful at loving ourselves. <u>Unless we are able to love ourselves, we never become good at loving others</u>. I have occasionally encountered undergraduates who denied this, but it's unlikely that any adults with decades of experience would be inclined to deny it. Does any adult seriously think that mastering the art of loving may be accidental? Since loving involves at least *relatively selfless giving rather than selfish taking*, it requires us persistently to give of ourselves. Unless we love ourselves, how would that be possible?

So I encourage you to think about loving yourself. Mastering the art of loving others requires mastering the art of loving yourself. What would you do, ideally, to take care of yourself and promote your own genuine happiness or well-being?

Isn't the obvious starting point our **bodies** (physical forms)? Being ill, injured, dismembered, or in pain are obstructions to happiness. Similarly, it's difficult to think of ourselves as being genuinely happy if we are very old, weak, and infirm. I'm not claiming that those who are extremely elderly, for example, cannot be masters of the art of loving; I'm only claiming that mastering the art of loving is much easier when we are physically whole, healthy, and vigorous. Ensuring that we eat well, exercise well, sleep well, and manage stress well are all ways of taking good care of ourselves physically, of loving ourselves, of being kind to ourselves. By way of contrast, abusing our bodies is the opposite of loving (caring for, tending) them.

We also have **feelings**. Some are pleasant. Some are unpleasant. Others are neutral. It's difficult to think of ourselves as being genuinely happy or flourishing if we are enduring intense, unpleasant feelings. Such feelings obstruct genuine happiness. When we have such feelings, we naturally want to heal them by transforming them into better feelings. Healing or dissolving unpleasant feelings is another important way of loving ourselves.

We also have **perceptions**. They are how we learn about the so-called "external" world. Sages have been telling us for thousands of years that incorrect perceptions cause suffering. Modern psychologists have repeatedly demonstrated that perceptions are not reliable channels that yield undistorted views of reality; instead, they are heavily influenced by our thoughts, our conceptual systems, our understanding (and, so, our expectations of what we anticipate perceiving). In other words, it's simply false that "seeing is believing"; instead, we see something when we believe it. It's as if perception yields so much information that it's necessary for us to filter and select it, to interpret it according to narratives or stories we accept. If it's dark and I fear snakes, I may panic before turning up the light and realizing that I am really looking at a thick rope. This is why witnesses to an accident often really see the unfolding of different events. These are simple examples of why it is always wise to question the accuracy of our perceptions.

Rejecting misleading perceptions is a third important way of loving ourselves.

This obviously relates to our ideas, our thoughts, judgments, or beliefs, and our theories (interconnected networks of thoughts, judgments, or beliefs). Such **mental formations** may have a lot or only a little to do with reality. The more attached to them we are, the more we live in our heads, the more we confuse what we believe with what is real, the more disconnected we become from reality. Our "surrealities" are often quite different from reality. Furthermore, we are also heavily influenced by the accepted views of collective consciousness, in other words, by the thoughts we have picked up from others in our culture. When we act unthoughtfully on the basis of such views, the result is human history, which is a history of madness or, as Churchill put it, "one damn thing after another." For example, in the twentieth century concluded a few years ago, it's been estimated by some scholars that over 100,000,000 humans beings died violently at the hands of other human beings. While the exact number is unknowable, it is very, very large. If that wasn't madness, there is no madness! One of the very best ways of loving ourselves is getting rid of unwholesome mental formations. They distort how we think about reality and make doing well either accidental or impossible.

There is also **consciousness** (awareness) itself. It may seem unusual to talk about loving ourselves by taking good care of our consciousness, but there's a specific way of doing that that is underappreciated. In the last three thousand or so years, writing has become ubiquitous. Literacy has enabled human beings to create many marvelous achievements such as the rise of cities and the greatly enhanced productivity made possible by the specialization of tasks. Yet the rise of literacy has had a price that too few of us have noticed, namely, it has enabled us to live more in our thoughts by cutting us off from the nonhuman world of our prehistoric ancestors. (David Abram has clearly articulated this in his brilliant book <u>The Spell of the Sensuous</u>.) It's as if we have become slaves to the literacy that separates us from the nonhuman world. What better way of loving ourselves is there than correcting that imbalance? The reason is that separation is always the cause of suffering and, by correcting that imbalance, we are diminishing the separation between ourselves and that natural world. To diminish separation is always to love. <u>To love is to promote union or re-union.</u>

If so, then we are living physical bodies who have feelings, perceptions, mental formations, and consciousness. That is hardly a complete understanding of human being, but any understanding that ignores one of those elements would be incomplete. It's a practical understanding. Furthermore, a complete understanding of human being is unnecessary for understanding the nature of authentic loving and practicing it better.

<u>Loving actions are healing actions, behaviors that reduce separation</u>. They automatically produce greater union or re-union. They automatically reduce suffering (discontent, dissatisfaction, unease, sorrow, <u>dukkha</u>).

There's no controversy about this. If I am ill and you successfully nurse me back to health, you have benefitted me by helping my body to heal. Nursing is a loving action. It's why we value the profession of nursing. You would have befriended me. Similarly, if you are angry or afraid and I reassure you by holding your hand and successfully help you to diminish the power of the negative emotions that are afflicting you, I have benefitted you by helping you to release your anger or fear. I would have befriended you. This kind of counseling is also a loving action. It's why we value the profession of counseling. Counselors befriend their clients. So nurses and counselors are like paid friends; we pay them to love us.

In this way it is natural to think of *friendship as the paradigm of loving.* Genuine friends (as opposed to paid friends) work to benefit each other without reward; if you are my friend, you work to benefit me, and, if I am your friend, I work to benefit you. Friends give to each other by understanding what is good for each other and promoting it. Ideally, they do it without either wanting or expecting anything in return. (If they did it while wanting or expecting something it return, they wouldn't be genuine friends but paid friends.)

Whether or not you agree that friendship is the paradigm of a loving relationship, it's impossible to understand the art of loving without understanding friendship. It turns out that, in the western tradition, Aristotle gave what has come to be understood as the best account of friendship, so it's important to consider his major ideas at least briefly. His ideas, though, did not come out of nowhere. He was a student of the first great philosopher of the western tradition, Plato. The right way to begin to understand Aristotle's ideas on loving is to understand the similarity and differences between his theory of loving and Plato's.

While Plato and Aristotle are the greatest thinkers from the western tradition, the Buddha is the greatest thinker from the eastern tradition. His account of reality is, I suggest, better than either Plato's or Aristotle's. If so, it's not surprising that his account of loving is superior to theirs as well. You can decide for yourself whether or not to agree with me. *Since loving relationships are important, why go through life without familiarizing yourself with the chief ideas about loving advocated by the three greatest philosophers?*

I consider Plato's theory of loving in the next chapter and Aristotle's in the chapter after that. These don't even pretend to be scholarly treatments. Instead, let's just articulate and evaluate some of their chief ideas about loving. Why? According to the great love scholar Irving Singer, "In the philosophy of love . . . every discussion must *start* with Plato."

If you are unfamiliar with philosophy, don't let the discipline intimidate you. To be a philosopher is to be a lover of wisdom. In other words, all philosophers are trying to do is to live better. If you are serious about living better, then you, too, are already a philosopher.

Some philosophers are unsuccessful in their quest and some are successful. Sages are successful philosophers. (In religious contexts, the word 'saints' is often used to refer to sages.) **Sages are the greatest lovers.** If you want to understand loving in order to practice it better, that's because you consider it wise to be loving, to love more like sages love. My intention in this book is to encourage you and help you to do that.

I hope to convince you that, while there is a lot of wisdom in what both Plato and Aristotle understand about loving, they share a fundamental flaw, which the Buddha's account overcomes, that is very instructive. Anyone who notices that flaw automatically becomes predisposed to becoming a better lover.

3. Plato on Loving

To think is to judge. To judge is to conceptualize, to use concepts (principles of classification) to sort (categorize, classify, divide, separate) things (objects, forms). For example, we think or say "that is an oak tree" or "this shirt is blue" or "it's good that she did that."

Concepts are arranged in hierarchies or conceptual frameworks according to generality. For example, it's logically impossible to answer the question, "What is a good human being?" without first answering the question, "What is a human being?" If we don't understand what human beings are, it's impossible to sort them into those who are good and those who aren't. Similarly, it's logically impossible to answer the question, "What is a human being?" without first answering the question, "What is a being?" If we don't understand what beings are, it's impossible to sort them into those that are human and those that aren't. So the question, "What is a being?" is logically more fundamental than the question, "What is a human being?" The question, "What is a human being?" is logically more fundamental than the question, "What is a good human being?"

Unless we are clear about the logically fundamental concepts, it's impossible to be anything except confused about the logically less fundamental concepts. This explains why most people are confused. They have failed to attend with sufficient care to the fundamental concepts.

(Don't confuse the notion of importance with the notion of logical fundamentality. The question, "What is a good human being?" may well be more important than the question, "What is a being?" even though it is less fundamental.)

It took me a long time to realize that <u>there are two fundamentally different conceptual frameworks for understanding loving.</u> Let's call them the "western" and the

21

"eastern." Which one we adopt will determine how we understand loving. I present both in this book, and you may select the one you think is best. (I argue that one is preferable to the other, but it's up to you to judge for yourself whether my argument is sound. If it is, you'll agree with me; if it isn't, you won't. At a minimum, by thinking it through for yourself you will clarify your understanding.)

Plato was the first great philosopher in the western tradition.

There were, though, important philosophers before him. The three most important were Parmenides of Elea, Heraclitus, and Socrates, who was Plato's own teacher.

Parmenides was a monist; he thought that reality or what-is is one substance. The truth, he argues, is that it is ungenerated and indestructible. Growth and decay are unreal, mere appearances. Furthermore, there is no unreality; what is unreal is absolutely inconceivable and unknowable. Also, there are no degrees of reality. What-is is single, indivisible, and homogeneous. It is perfect from every angle; its mass is equally matched in every way like that of a ball.

Heraclitus thought that reality is a multitude of substances. Everything flows. It's not easy to understand because, contrary to what we expect, whatever opposes produces a benefit. The true nature of forms is concealed. "Lovers of wisdom must open their minds to very many things indeed . . . There is a greater need to extinguish arrogance than a blazing fire." It's a new sun every day.

Socrates was Plato's hero. Socrates's chief concern was living the good life. Plato made Socrates the chief character in the dialogues he wrote. He has Socrates say, "the most important thing is not life, but the good life . . . the unexamined life is not worth living for man." Socrates became a martyr for philosophy.

The reason that Plato was the first great philosopher in the western tradition was that he was the first to ask and argue for answers to all the fundamental questions. Those are the questions dealing with reality, apprehension, and morality. Panayot Butchvarov: "In addition to asking what is real, the question of metaphysics [ontology], and what do we really know, the question of epistemology, we ask, what are we to do, the question of ethics . . ."

While most of his predecessors like Parmenides and Heraclitus had been primarily concerned with questions about the nature of reality and our apprehension of it and one, Socrates, had been primarily concerned with morality, Plato was concerned about all three fundamental domains. He correctly thought that philosophy begins with wondering about them and that "philosophy is the greatest of the arts." Our answers to questions of value, our answers to questions about what we should value and how we should live are important. They are useless if unsupported; they must be grounded upon more fundamental questions about the apprehension of reality.

There are two other preliminary points to make about doing philosophy. First, since we don't know who the best philosophers are, it's necessary as well as important to think things through for ourselves. Either we do that or we remain confused. So please forget focusing on the lives of the great philosophers; instead, focus on the subject matter. Plato himself put it this way: "in every line of life the stupid are many and worthless, the serious are few and worth everything . . . Do not trouble about those who practice philosophy, whether they are good or bad; but examine the thing itself well and carefully." Second, the only presupposition required for doing philosophy is the practical belief that practicing philosophy may be beneficial. Panayot Butchvarov: "For philosophers, everything is in question, including all disciplines, even their own. Theirs is an inquiry without presuppositions, neither of subject matter nor of method."

Plato's account of the nature of love is primarily found in his dialogue Symposium. The human search for love is a search for a good wholeness, a valuable unity. Separated, individual human beings are incomplete and they naturally yearn for completeness. They search for completeness or wholeness, but it's not just that. It's that nothing would count as completeness or wholeness unless it were good (valuable, preferable). Furthermore, it cannot be perishable or, otherwise, grasping it would only be temporary and lasting satisfaction would be impossible. We desire perpetual possession of that good.

Human beings are naturally acquisitive (desiring, greedy). They always desire what they (correctly or incorrectly) think will be good.

Lovers learn by experience what works and what doesn't. Suppose, for example, that you have sexual desire to possess another person who is physically beautiful as well as being someone who also has what we might call a beautiful soul. These qualities are not limited to any one other person. Furthermore, at least physical beauty will not last in any one other person. So the ideal lover learns to go higher by learning to desire something less concrete and changeable to desiring something more abstract and enduring. This ascent eventually leads to the only entities that could satisfy our desire for perpetual possession, which are unchanging eternal objects of goodness, beauty, and reality. There may be one ultimate, timeless entity that is the best, the most beautiful, and the most real.

Words can only point to it. It is beyond conceptualization. Absolute goodness/beauty/reality neither begins to exist nor ceases to exist. It is not beautiful in parts and ugly in other parts. It is not beautiful at one time and ugly at another. It is not beautiful in one place and ugly at another. Its beauty does not vary with the status of those who behold it. Everything lesser that is beautiful is beautiful because it participates in Beauty itself, but their generation and destruction have no impact on it. Similar remarks about its goodness and reality are applicable.

For Plato, what is eternal is more real than the changeable, temporal physical individual bodies that may temporarily participate in them. Why might this be true?

Consider, for example, a blue shirt that comes into being, exists (for a while), and eventually ceases to be. What makes it blue? Its participation in blueness, which is eternal. The shirt is a temporal, changeable object whereas its color is an unchanging timeless object. While the statement that "this shirt is blue" may be true at one time and not at another time, the statement that "Blueness is a color" is timelessly true. (A blind person may be ignorant of it, but that only means that the blind person is ignorant. It doesn't mean that it's false that blueness is a color.) In a way, then, eternal objects confront us with more force than temporal objects, which may explain why Plato thinks them more real than any spatiotemporal individuals that participate in them.

For him, to be a human being is to be caught uncomfortably between two domains, namely, the temporal and the eternal. The living flesh that is our bodies exists in the ceaseless flux of becoming, whereas our ability to apprehend "Forms" enables us to participate in that which is eternal.

The ideal lover who ascends the ladder of love to its highest level becomes as immortal as it is possible for a human being to become by directly experiencing what is absolute with an unfettered soul.

The sage, the successful philosopher who is wise, contemplates a world of unchanging reality, goodness, and beauty. This is **the ultimate union**, the overcoming of all separation. Because of this constant companionship with what is divine, his or her life will naturally reproduce that order and, so, become as godlike as it is possible for human beings to become.

This is why the Socrates in Plato's dialogues says multiple times that his lord is love and, furthermore, that it is the only subject he understands.

Notice that this account emphasizes a perpetual possession, in other words, a radically changed state from our normal state of frequent dissatisfaction. Since suffering is always caused by separation, there is enormous value in Plato's emphasis on union. The possibility that opens up here is the possibility of living without suffering by living in perpetual union. If that is a genuine possibility, how are we to achieve it?

Clearly it is not by physical or sexual union. That's far too temporary. Loving, for Plato, is all about desiring a wholeness or completeness that is good. This cannot possibly be sexual union, although those who are beginners in love might mistake it for that. It's sufficient to point out that the satisfaction from even a successful sexual union is fleeting.

What Plato is encouraging us to understand is the value of a particular kind of 'arete', which is usually translated as 'excellence' or 'virtue.' It is only by living an examined life that one develops the particular kind of excellence in question. The purpose of living an examined life is not to spend life ceaselessly searching but to live well, to become wise, to enjoy the fruits of living an examined life. A human being who doesn't live an examined life is not living a life worth living; he or she has no chance of living well.

A sage has <u>arête</u>. He or she has achieved salvation. It begins with a self-centered quest to live better but ends with such a radical transformation that it cannot even be described in words (see the allegory of the cave in the <u>Republic</u>). In terms of benefitting oneself and benefitting others, Plato argues in the <u>Republic</u> that <u>genuinely benefitting yourself will automatically genuinely benefit others</u>. It may help to think of it as the enlargement of one's self concept to include others.

Singer identifies a fundamental difficulty in Plato's account of loving. On the one hand, human beings (and, for Plato, all other living beings) are motivated by a desire for a wholeness that is good, but, on the other hand, nothing can satisfy this desire for perpetual satisfaction within the domain of ceaseless flux in which human beings live.

This is why Plato thinks that only sages, successful philosophers, can be great lovers. Only they have broken beyond the domain of the temporal to experience the eternal directly.

I actually think that, properly interpreted [see my Getting Things Done], Plato is right about this. However, the key to understanding it is not to emphasize reasoning about eternal objects (or, for example, mathematicians would be sages!), but to emphasize the limitless expansion of the self concept, which amounts to letting go of it (since it ceases to be a principle of separation). In other words, although it can help to clear the way (as I hope happens to you as you read this book), it is not more and better thinking that produces great lovers. Learning how to become a great lover involves learning how to drop thinking altogether.

Why? **Thinking separates whereas loving unites.** Because it involves overcoming separation, it's impossible to think your way to becoming a great lover.

Notice that it is logically impossible to think unity. Since thinking requires separation and there is no separation in unity, thinking cannot grasp unity. Thought cannot grasp loving!

I'm not arguing against the value of good thinking. That would be idiotic. Good thinking provides solutions to important problems.

I'm arguing that even good thinking has limited usefulness. Why this is so will become clearer as we proceed.

Let's consider the account of loving offered by Plato's greatest student.

4. Aristotle on Loving

Like all the ancient Greek philosophers, Aristotle thinks of a loving relationship or encounter between human beings as one between persons, which he takes to be two continuants. (A "continuant" is a temporal entity that exists at two or more consecutive times.) He presupposes the self/nonself or self/other distinction. For example, if you and I are friends, you and I are different persons who stand in a certain relationship, namely, the friendship relation.

On the other hand, Aristotle says in the <u>Nichomachean Ethics</u>, which is his main teaching on loving, that a friend is like another self: "your friend . . . is another yourself."

Aristotle thinks that in most friendships the friends are just using each other. These are "utility" friendships. If I befriend you because you are useful to me (because, for example, you are able to increase my enjoyment or security or prosperity), then I am using you for my own purposes(s); if you are also using me for your own purpose(s), then we have a utility friendship. As long as there's no deception involved and a minimum amount of time and effort is spent on it, there's nothing necessarily wrong with a utility friendship. (It would, though, in my view usually be wrong to use another merely as a means to my own end(s) without reciprocity.) Pleasure friendships, including ordinary sex affairs, are just a variety of utility friendships.

Genuine friendships are "complete." Think of the friendship you have with your best friend. **Complete friends** do not merely use each other or merely enjoy sharing activities; they promote each other's good. Ideally, each should work hard, selflessly, and regularly to promote what is best for the other. Aristotle thinks it proper for complete friends to live together. Only morally good people can engage in complete friendships, and the friends must be roughly equal in goodness (moral worth or value). Because complete friends deeply understand each other and constantly challenge each other to live better, it's like a win/win competition in which each person becomes more morally excellent. Complete friendships require a lot of time and honest communication for their creation, and they are abiding, relatively long lasting. Because they require sustained effort, even a morally excellent person who is lucky will enjoy very few complete friendships in a lifetime.

In theory, an excellent person who is "blessedly happy and self-sufficient" may not need friends, but, in practice, such a person does need friends. Why? It's not because of neediness. Though the sage does not need others to benefit himself or herself, "the excellent person will need people for him to benefit."

Friendship is a self-conscious "reciprocated goodwill," a "mutual loving," and "loving is like production," in other words, friendships are deliberated created. A friendship is an acting rather than a "being acted on," in other words, befriending someone is doing something and not having something happen to you. It's a giving rather than a taking. It benefits another. The sage enjoys acting excellently by benefitting other morally excellent friends.

What's the real difference between utility friendships and complete friendships? The former are conditional; the latter are unconditional. Both friends must love unconditionally in order for there to be a complete friendship.

Utility friendships (including utility sex affairs) aren't about love at all. They are nothing but bargains or business arrangements. This doesn't mean that they are immoral. All it means is that they are not examples of genuine loving. What may be called "conditional love" isn't really love at all.

In loving unconditionally, what one is doing, benefitting the other, is primary. Ideally, and this is going beyond

Aristotle but it's compatible with his account, one's self concept disappears; there's just the optimal or flow experience of giving itself. As Nietzsche points out, only sages radiate love; it's as if with them there's a superabundance or overflowing of goodness.

Since it takes an extraordinary amount of moral excellence, which comes from character development [that is really ego attrition] even to be capable of unconditional love, it should not be surprising that complete friendships occur infrequently.

There's a lot of practical wisdom in Aristotle's account. Nobody in the entire western philosophic tradition has produced a more influential account of friendship.

For example, it's easy to extend them to sex affairs, which always come up in discussions of loving. Just as most friendships are merely utility friendships, aren't most sex affairs governed by mutual need satisfaction? Ordinary sex affairs are nothing but extensions of utility friendships, utility friends with sexual benefits. When pleasure is exchanged and the male gains respect and the female gains "love," that's merely a rational bargain.

It's an open question whether their benefits in pleasure, companionship, social status, and the like are worth their costs in terms of time and effort. They are naturally unstable. They almost always inevitably increase emotional and sometimes physical suffering. Like intoxicating substances, they often feel good temporarily while really only distracting us from working through our own dissatisfactions directly. An ordinary sex affair is the inevitable outcome if even one of the lovers is needy, in other words, not self sufficient. They are started for all sorts of foolish reasons such as attempting to overcome loneliness, trying to increase one's standing in society, trying to satisfy a desire to parent another or to be parented by another, falling in love (lust), and so on. It's no wonder that divorce, infidelity, promiscuity, and serial monogamy are so prevalent.

Mustn't one be both skillful and lucky to emerge from the game of romance even slightly ahead?

A "grand encounter" is a sex affair that is an extension of a complete friendship. They necessarily involve sustained effort and intense, egoless caring. They presuppose the highest respect for oneself and for the other. They take a lot of time and skillful effort to create and sustain, but they tend to be relatively enduring. They occur only between morally good people similar in excellence. One characteristic of someone who has a morally good character is not being needy; in other words, it's being capable of living well in solitude. This immediately disqualifies most people from ever enjoying a grand encounter. Since they require mutual sexual attraction and complete friendships don't, they are even more infrequent than complete friendships. (I myself have never experienced one, and a sufficient reason for that is that I have not yet become successful enough at ego attrition – and I may never be.)

Whereas Plato thinks that eternal objects are more real than temporal objects, Aristotle argues that Plato's view is backwards. For Aristotle, to resume the blue shirt example, the shirt itself is primary whereas its color is secondary. As for Plato's ideas about abstract objects like Blueness, one of Aristotle's powerful critical questions is simply this: is Blueness itself blue? If it is not blue, then that explains nothing about the blueness of the shirt. If, on the other hand, it is blue, then what explains the truth of the predication that Blueness itself is blue? It would seem that there must be some other level of abstract objects that would explain the participation of Blueness in being blue – and that leads to a vicious infinite regress. If so, Plato's theory about eternal "Forms" explains nothing. Again, for Aristotle, temporal changeable individuals are the primary existents – not timeless ones.

Despite the practical value of his account of loving, Aristotle's account of loving is theoretically insufficient. In fact, all accounts that are fundamentally similar to Plato's or Aristotle's – and that implicates most accounts from the western tradition up until the time of Nietzsche – are theoretically insufficient. Even from a practical viewpoint, it's helpful to understand why. I explain why in the next chapter and sketch an account that is theoretically sufficient after that.

5: The Foundational Problem

There's a serious foundational problem about any understanding of loving that sees it as a relation between two continuant persons. It's possible that this problem can be overcome, but I don't think so. If so, there should be a fundamental shift in anyone's conceptual framework who takes lovers to be continuant persons.

Over twenty years ago I considered writing a book about friendship. I started thinking and actually began writing it. I hit a brick wall and stopped.

The foundational problem or brick wall that confronted me was this: if loving is a relation between two persons (who are continuant substrata) that is designed to result in union by overcoming separation, **loving is impossible!** Either that or the persons wouldn't be lovers.

In other words, suppose that person S and person P are friends who love each other. If love is the overcoming of separation, then either S and P cannot be successful friends or S must cease being S and P must cease being P to become one union. It makes no sense to posit both union and separation simultaneously.

The solution, which required years for me really to understand, is that, since people are not separate, independent substrata, **authentic love is possible**. What the block is, perhaps not surprisingly, is getting stuck thinking of the other as separate. Aristotle got that wrong. A friend is not like another yourself; a friend is not something separate. In a genuine friendship, a friend is me! In genuine love, the "other" is not other.

If it helps, you may think of expanding your self concept to include another person. If you take anything outside your skin to be really important to you, you already understand this. Suppose, for example, as some parents do, you identify so much with your children that, if they died, you would die or that you are willing to sacrifice your life for theirs. That would be an everyday expansion of a self concept to include other people. There's no genuine love without union.

Both the historical Buddha and the great Scottish philosopher David Hume advocated what has come to be known as a nonsubstance ontology. Are individuals nothing but clusters of qualities or is there something more (a substratum) to individuals that clusters those qualities together? (Many other recent philosophers like Bradley and Butchvarov also advocate a nonsubstance ontology.)

A nonsubstance ontology goes against the way that we ordinarily think and talk. In that sense, it is counter-intuitive. It may well be, however, that the way we ordinarily think and talk is inadequate and misleading. Everyone agrees that individuals are clusters of qualities (properties, commonalities). For example, my dining room table is oak, hard, thirty inches tall, and has a top that is 40 inches by 62 inches. Other individuals may be made of oak. Other individuals may be hard. Other things may have that same height. And so on. What is unique about that table?

Substance ontologists claim that it has a unique substratum that distinguishes it from all similar tables and all other things. (Most substance ontologists agree with Aristotle who emphasizes that substances are continuants. Some substance ontologists take substrata to be momentary particulars that are devoid of qualities [hence, "bare particulars"] that are mere individuators.) For example, if I take a saw and cut a chunk out of that table top, would it be the same table? Yes, says Aristotle, although it would have a (slightly) different shape. In that way, substances are supposed to survive qualitative change.

Similarly, are you the same person you were ten years ago despite the fact that your weight may have changed, your understanding has changed, etc.? It's natural to think so.

That's partly, I think, because of language. Sentences have subjects and predicates. I am cold. That table is hard. She is beautiful. Water is wet.

When there's thought or talk about myself such as "I am cold" or "I want a drink of water," what does "I" really denote? It's not a physical body nor a part of a physical body nor a bodily sensation. It's not an emotion. It's not a thought. What is it?

Would you still be you if you lost all your memories? If so, this suggests that you may be a set of thoughts, your autobiographical narrative. At least that had a beginning, has a middle (now), and, presumably, will have an end. Do you identify with your personal story? At least it does seem unique to you. Nobody else has the exact same story.

After all, your very name is unchanging! This is an instance of the general truth that words, concepts, and judgments abide in the sense that they are always available to think. On the other hand, are you really satisfied by thinking that you are nothing but a set of ephemeral thoughts? Words, concepts, and judgments are unnatural in the sense that they are merely human creations; in that sense, they are unlike ever-changing mountains, lakes, and wolves.

The foundational problem comes from being unable to think of an individual without any qualities. Since the table is not its shape, we have to distinguish its shape from what has it. After all, other objects may have the same shape. The same goes for all its other qualities. (This leads to what philosophers call the problem of individuation.) So it's important to separate substrata (whether they are taken to be momentary "bare particulars" or continuants) from their qualities.

Substance ontologists claim that substrata are real. Sorry, I have no clue what they are talking about. Perhaps you are unlike me in this respect, but I am unable to think of individuals without qualities. I understand why some philosophers want to believe in them, but I'm clueless when it comes to understanding what they are talking about.

If so, the idea of thinking of loving as being a relation of friendship between, say, me and you is incoherent. What is the substratum that is supposed to cluster your qualities? What is the substratum that is supposed to cluster my qualities? Furthermore, is the relation between them, the friendship relation, "internal" to us or "external" to us and real as some third entity (in addition to me and you)? (This leads to what philosophers call the problem of understanding relational qualities. Relational qualities like leftness or betweenness have two or more subjects whereas monadic qualities such as blueness or rectangularity have one subject.) Bradley argues that the very concept of an individual is an "abstraction" and, as such, unreal, in other words, not something that possesses identity.

There are lots and lots of fundamental issues here. Fortunately, improving our skill at loving does not require solving them all. I mention them primarily to encourage you to wonder about the adequacy of any substance ontology.

My secondary intention here is to encourage you to wonder about the deleterious effects that literacy has had on our thinking. Do you think that only human beings speak? Or are you also able to listen to the talk coming from mountains, lakes, and wolves? If you are stuck listening only to other humans, you may be very pleased with what follows because your world may become immensely richer.

However, it is likely that you will feel some resistance from the mind, possibly a great deal of resistance. The mind is great at generating questions. It insists that you answer them all before letting go of its fondest views. If you follow that course, however, you'll never break free from thought. If you let yourself remain stuck, you'll simply usually miss experiencing the more-than-human world with all its richness. After all, it is our natural home.

Please try fully to absorb the thought that the mind is limited to conceptual understanding and you aren't. Judgments, thoughts, are the stuff of the mind. Since thinking requires using concepts and since concepts are principles of separation, it is impossible for the mind to think unity because there is no separation in unity. Concepts are always dualistic: either something falls under a concept or it doesn't. If you identify solely with the mind, you will stay stuck living dualistically. What's wrong with that? **All dissatisfaction (suffering, discontent, unease, sorrow, imbalance, misery, <u>dukkha</u>) comes from separation. If you identify solely with the mind, it becomes impossible to overcome dissatisfaction.** You are, almost certainly without intending to do so, condemning yourself to continued dissatisfaction.

The **good news** is that it is not necessary to do that. Insofar as you let go of identifying solely with the mind, you are opening yourself up to the direct experience of unity, which is the overcoming of separation and, so, dissatisfaction. **Dissatisfaction is optional**.

This opening from thought to no-thought, from thinking to awareness, from being unbalanced to being balanced, is inclusive rather than exclusive. It does not require permanently giving up thinking; instead, it involves opening a critical dimension to consciousness. To think incessantly is to use the ability to think improperly; to think only when necessary is to use the ability to think properly. It's not necessary to misuse the mind.

So the usual problem isn't thinking itself: it's attachment to thinking, compulsive thinking. When you let go of solely identifying with the mind, what you are doing is letting go of slavery in favor of freedom.

Making this shift from thought to awareness is critical to mastering the art of loving. It may be understood as expanding what you identify with until you identify with everything and your self concept ceases to become a concept. That's the most important thesis in this book. If you take one idea away from reading this book, it should be the idea you take. *Mastering the art of loving requires thorough awareness that you are more than just the mind.* Your nature as a human being may, in other words, be much richer than you previous thought.

Let's discuss how to make this transition easier.

6: Getting Unstuck

Imagine yourself as a large helium-filled balloon that is tied to the earth with ropes. What do you have to do to soar freely through the air? Cut the ropes. Since you are both stuck and naturally free, it's only a matter of getting rid of what is obstructing you from rising. Living well as a balloon is possible for you if you will cut through the obstructions.

You are naturally free as a human being. You always have been. The only reason you are not soaring is because you are stuck. You are stuck by thoughts generated by the mind. Since you are naturally free, it's only a matter of getting rid of what is obstructing you from rising. Living well as a human being is possible for you if you will cut through the obstructions.

It's impossible in one book to cut through all possible thoughts that may be obstructing you. However, by cutting through some of the major ones, you'll quickly understand how the process works. In the future, whenever you feel restrained, seriously examine the thought that is restraining you and that restraint will wither and dissolve.

Restraining thoughts may be understood as objections and each has a satisfactory reply. However, the replies, ultimately, are not conceptual. As the sage Lao-tzu states in the opening of his <u>Taoteching</u>, the way that can be told or talked about is not the way, the way called 'the way' is not the way. That being noted, we may now emulate him by going on and talking about it.

OBJECTION 1: According to a nonsubstance ontology, I have no structure as an individual, but that makes no sense. If I am not a substratum holding my qualities together, what is doing the clustering of my qualities? I am not merely a list of qualities; I'm a unified cluster of them.

REPLY 1: The reason that a nonsubstance ontology doesn't make sense to you is that you are stuck believing in a substance ontology. Notice the structure of the argument behind your own position: Since I cannot think how qualities (which are similar to pins) could not be clustered without an underlying substratum (pin cushion), it *must be* there.

The only way to know the nature of reality is to apprehend it directly. If all you do is adopt a conceptual framework and then perceive reality in accordance with it, all you have done is provided yourself with contaminated perception. Instead of going to reality and attempting to find what your theory says must be there, start with a conceptually neutral apprehension and build your conceptual framework from that.

This objection reminds me of a similar one raised against physicists between Newton and Einstein who thought that ether must fill the universe because their conceptual framework required it. Of course, despite attempting to detect it, they never did because it never existed. That demonstrated the inadequacy of their theory. Once the theory (the conceptual framework) improved, the need to posit the existence of ether evaporated.

Furthermore, even if you are an individual who is nothing but a cluster of qualities, it is possible to understand that clustering without positing the existence of quality-less substrata [See Butchvarov's Being Qua Being, chapter 8.] Once the theory improves, the need to posit the existence of substrata evaporates.

Actually, it's the supposition that you are an individual separate from everything else that is the root of the problem. That view makes us all rather like bumper cars in an amusement arcade occasionally colliding into each other and bumping off to go their separate ways without any unifying connections. Stay stuck on that fundamental assumption and understanding authentic loving will remain impossible.

Furthermore, it's almost certain that you have spontaneously experienced moments that enabled you to experience direct awareness without thought. These are moments that take one's conceptual breath away. Even such fundamental concepts as time and self drop away momentarily.

For example, has it ever happened that you have awakened in the morning and just enjoyed some pure awareness until the usual heavy avalanche of thoughts overwhelmed the experience? Have you ever unexpectedly observed great beauty and were stunned into silent awe? Have you ever mastered a craft or a musical instrument or a sport skill such that, suddenly and unexpectedly, while you were doing it for the umpteenth time "it" happened and you just became what you were doing?

These moments, and other like them, are natural, spontaneous openings to the more-than-human world beyond concepts. Reality includes that world as well as the human-created world.

Reality is the obstructed obvious. The obstructions are concepts, which deaden life. Drop the obstructions and directly experience reality without distortions and immediately begin feeling more alive. Or, if you prefer, just keep sticking slavishly to your favorite conceptual framework and, so, continue the dissatisfaction until death.

OBJECTION 2: This would mean that the everyday ego is a delusion, but that's absurd. So this cannot be correct.

REPLY 2: Nobody denies the existence of an everyday ego (ordinary self, ego/I). Indeed, for practical purposes, we've see that it consists of a cluster of corporeality, feelings, perceptions, mental formations, and consciousness.

Each of us has an everyday self concept, a dividing line between what we take ourselves to be and everything that we don't take ourselves to be. Notice, though, that there is no agreement on the extent or range of this concept! Philosophers have discussed this a lot and there is no consensus.

That's because it's a vague concept. That's not necessarily bad. Most everyday concepts are vague; if they weren't, they would be much less useful.

The important point is that **there doesn't seem to be any unchanging, autonomous entity behind experiencing who is having the experiences**. If we introspect and look deeply enough inside, we do seem to be empty. We then cling to our life stories, which are just a string of thoughts, and identify with those thoughts. It is precisely such clinging that always creates our discontent. Why?

No judgment or thought can be the whole truth. Since thoughts require concepts and since concepts separate, at most a thought can be partially true. If you string together a series of partial truths, do you arrive at the whole truth? No. All you have is a string of partial truths. Sages have made this point over and over again. A frozen fishing net cannot capture water.

Theories (views, accounts, stories) are built from thoughts. They never capture the whole truth. That's not what they are good for. What's their value? It's for making better decisions. If thoughts and theories help us to make better decisions, that's terrific. If they don't, chuck them. There's nothing sacred about them. Ultimately, they are just perspectives, points of view.

In other words, it's impossible think from thought to no-thought. To experience no-thought, drop attachment to all thoughts. Do that even for a moment, and you'll have a direct, though brief, glimpse of unobstructed reality. There's no other requirement.

OBJECTON 3: There is no entity without identity. Every form is what it is and is different from every other form. What you are saying violates this fundamental truth.

REPLY 3: It is a fundamental truth – for the mind! If you limit yourself to conceptual understanding, it's fine.

However, *non*conceptual understanding goes beyond conceptual understanding.

If so, this means that you are not only the mind. If you limit yourself to thinking conceptually, you must limit your self concept. The problem with doing that is that your self concept is unlimited; self is actually Self.

Although the following makes no sense to the mind it is nevertheless true that every form is not what it is and is the same as every other form and, so, it really is what it is. If you don't understand this, it's because you are thinking about it. Conceptual thinking can be very useful in dealing with (parts of) reality, but it is useless when it comes to understanding unity, which includes all reality. In other words, grasping reality conceptually always distorts it.

In Buddhism, for example, this is the significance of the word 'tathata' or 'thusness.'

The notion of a separate individual entity is itself a conceptual delusion. (Illusions are cases of experiencing something real incorrectly; delusions are cases of experiencing something unreal.) It's often called "ego delusion." If so, this explains why there's endless theorizing by concept-bound philosophers about the nature of the self.

What is real? Thus!

That's the right answer. Of course, concept-bound philosophers want more. Trying to help them, other philosophers who are not bound to concepts say things like "individuals are empty." This may just mean that individuals are empty of substrata. It's initially frightening to apply this to ourselves. Am I, too, empty? Don't be alarmed. Thich Nhat Hanh: "All concepts about emptiness are the enemies of emptiness."

Actually, for clear-headed conceptual understanding, identity judgments are decisions. Once any two apparently separate forms are identified, Butchvarov argues, their indiscernibility is enforceable. (In particular, the concept of reality or existence is itself empty. For example, it is not applied on the basis of any phenomenal quality because, if it were, there would never be any mistaken existential judgments and, of course, there are.) In other words, *there is more conceptual freedom than most people realize.*

What is required to understand ourselves is a conceptual reset. In fact, *it's possible to prove to yourself that a nonsubstance ontology is preferable to a substance ontology.* What's not possible is for me or anyone else to provide a conceptual proof. Signposts? Yes. Directions that might prove helpful? Yes. I provide both in this book. Conceptual proof? No.

What is required is freedom from compulsive conceptualizing. It's a kind of waking up. (Although I have written about this multiple times [in, for example,Getting Things Done], I'm not well-qualified to discuss it. Even if I were, conceptual discussions are of limited usefulness.)

What would genuine loving be between two people who have so awakened? Excellent question! Here's the answer: such love is . . . *thus*! In other words, there is no conceptual answer.

This, though, is not satisfying to the mind. Can't we do better? Yes. Why not turn to the eastern tradition of nonsubstance ontology and try to learn from it?

The modern philosopher Alfred North Whitehead once remarked that western philosophy has been a series of footnotes to Plato. This, of course, is an exaggeration, but its point is correct in that Plato did set the agenda. He was the greatest philosopher in that tradition and there could never be another like him.

Similarly, eastern philosophy has been a series of footnotes to the Buddha. Like Plato, the Buddha had predecessors. However, the Buddha set the agenda. He was the greatest philosopher in that tradition and there could never be another like him.

Unlike Plato, the Buddha didn't write any books. Still, his teachings were memorized and eventually redacted so that we are able to think through his teachings for ourselves by reading what he supposedly said.

There's an important point of similarity between the Buddha and Plato, namely, each wanted us to do philosophy for ourselves (as I am encouraging you to do as you read this book). Remember, as Umberto Eco put it, that books are "lazy machines." As Emerson said, "nothing is got for nothing." In other words, you gotta pay the price; nobody can pay your price for you.

Why do you think that Plato wrote dialogues? If he had just wanted us to memorize what he considered truth, he could have simply written monologues for his followers to ingest. Dialogues implicitly invite their audience to participate in the discussion. In fact, there are some dialogues in which Plato criticized his own theories. So at least part of his motivation in writing dialogues was to encourage us to lead lives of active examination.

One reason, perhaps, why the Buddha didn't write any books was because he didn't want his followers simply attaching to his views. He offered his teachings to many different people in many different places over a long 45 year teaching career. In his last words, he encouraged his followers to be diligent in leading lives of active examination, to uncover truth for themselves.

When the Buddha extended an invitation to others who wished to join his order, he'd say simply, "Come!" or "Come and see!" As Glenn Wallis points out, "Note that he does not require some sort of admission of faith or oath of loyalty. From the outset, he seems to be asking the follower to be open, probing, and discerning." In other words, the Buddha would want you to approach his teachings as a philosopher. I, too, invite you to do that.

7: The Buddha on Loving

Plato and Aristotle are the greatest two philosophers in the western tradition. Their ideas have been extremely influential. The third greatest thinker of early western philosophy was Plotinus, who was a neo-Platonic thinker.

After the rise of Christianity, naturally Christian theologians attempted to create a coherent conceptual framework for its ideas. They modified the conceptual framework already set in place by the earlier Greek philosophers to do so. The first great Christian thinker was Augustine, who was heavily influenced by Plotinus (and ultimately Plato) as well as Paul. The other great theologian of the western middle ages was Aquinas, who was an Aristotelian. (Most of Plato's dialogues were unknown to him.) Both Augustine and Aquinas were very influential and, so, it's impossible to understand western philosophy in the middle ages without understanding its Greek background.

Serious wisdom seeking in the modern era was inaugurated by Descartes who gave new answers to the questions raised by Augustine, Aquinas and other important medieval thinkers. So, at least indirectly, all the great modern philosophers such as Spinoza, Leibniz, Locke, Berkeley, Hume, Kant, and Hegel approached the fundamental questions with the presuppositions of a substance ontology that can be traced back to Plato and Aristotle. In the history of western philosophy, it's impossible to overestimate the influence of Plato and Aristotle.

The greatest philosopher in the eastern tradition, and I think in world history, was the Buddha.

One of the major reasons for preferring his ontology to that of Plato or Aristotle is that he thought that we were all of equal moral worth or value. From a moral point of view, the Buddha taught that human beings are all equally valuable, that we are all brothers and sisters, and provided the ontological and epistemological foundation for that view. In the west it was Christians who popularized this idea and it was adopted by all major medieval and modern western philosophers. For example, while neither Plato nor Aristotle even opposed slavery, the Buddha advocated the then radical notion that woman had the same moral worth as men.

Although the Buddha's chief motivation was, like Socrates, living well, he separates himself from the rest because his was the first nonsubstance ontology. His most distinctive and innovative thesis was his claim that all individuals are empty of a self. Understanding that claim is critical to understanding his project of eliminating dissatisfaction.

Distinguish pain from dissatisfaction. It may be true that all sentient beings experience pain at least occasionally. Pain has an evolutionary function. If you break your ankle and try walking on it, you'll experience pain. It's as if your body is signaling you to take a break from walking for a while until the bones heal. In fact, if you never felt pain, you'd probably accidently kill yourself.

Dissatisfaction (discontent, unease, suffering, sorrow, dukkha), on the other hand, is, according to the Buddha, optional. All human beings experience dissatisfaction of various kinds. If we are lucky, even if we don't experience much pain or illness, we grow old and die. As the Buddha puts it: "aging and death are rolling in on you." We are subject to aging, to "growing old, brokenness of teeth, greyness of hair, wrinkling of skin, decline of vitality, [and] degeneration of the faculties." Then there's mortality with the breakup and decay of the body.

What's the remedy? The Buddha claims that, if we take refuge in the three treasures, all dissatisfaction will disappear.

What are the three treasures? There are different ways to interpret them. They are best understood as (i) one's real nature, (ii) the Buddha's teachings, and (iii) fellow practitioners. I briefly explain below the Buddha's account of the self and what it is to be a practitioner. Let's initially focus on the basic conceptual framework that grounds his radical doctrine of emptiness.

Since sages, those who are noble, live without dissatisfaction and nothing else is required for living well, how should we understand sages and what should we do to become sages? Since sages are the only master lovers, this promises the solution to the problem of how to master the art of authentic loving.

The Buddha provides four truths for those who would become sages.

First, living is difficult, imperfect, flawed. We experience discontent, sorrow, and dissatisfaction. Sometimes our suffering is acute; other times it is mild. Either way, our lives are persistently and pervasively unsatisfactory. There is even sadness in the midst of our happiest moments to which we cling because we realize they will soon end. Life humbles and humiliates us. We experience illness and decay. We suffer from the infirmities of aging. Soon we shall die. None of our loving encounters are permanent. We cannot control our own destinies.

Second, it is ego delusion that causes the egocentric attachments and aversions that create dissatisfaction. Our narcissistic cravings are what cause our dissatisfaction. As we continually ask of the world what it cannot give, as we incessantly try to control what cannot be controlled, as we incessantly are buffeted by one obsessive thirst after another, we hurt. We think that we are over here, that what we desire what is over there and that gaining it will cause our dissatisfaction to end. This separation between the way the world is and the way we would like it to be creates dissatisfaction.

Third, it's possible to eliminate dissatisfaction by eliminating what is causing it. Once we successfully practice ego attrition, once we work successfully to undermine our selfish desires, we discover that we lack nothing. Once we realize that we lack nothing, all egocentric thirsts vanish. Once we successfully counter all the normal psychological conditioning that is keeping us in bondage, we free ourselves.

Fourth, the way to liberation is the eightfold path or way that everyone who becomes a sage walks: right view, right thinking, right speech, right action, right livelihood, right diligence, right mindfulness, and right concentration. These are synergistic; they work together to alleviate dissatisfaction.

The key to all eight is the training (disciplining, purifying, emptying) of the mind. Sages shape the mind "[a]s irrigators lead water where they want, as archers make their arrows straight, as carpenters carve wood." **The fundamental choice is stark: either train the mind or fail to live well.** Short of training the mind, nothing can be done to live well: "no amount of penance can help a person whose mind is not purified."

So how are we to train the mind?

According to the Buddha, there is only one way: meditation. "There can be no meditation for those who are not wise, and no wisdom for those who do not meditate." Meditation purifies the mind by antidoting such poisons as acquisitiveness, anger, and delusions. These are what create our troubles. Since dissatisfactions are optional, it is foolish to live in thrall to them.

Instead, follow the lead of sages whose lives are characterized by clarity, insight, and present-moment mindfulness. This is "nirvana." It's available here and now, in the present moment. To find out for yourself, simply do what it takes to become a sage.

What's that? It's dropping all thoughts. Do that for a single moment, and you'll directly experience your true nature. It's that simple.

How? Train the mind. Instead of letting thoughts take charge of you, you take charge of them. Though it's simple, "hard it is to train the mind."

Therefore, the life of a sage does not involve gaining anything that the rest of us lack. Nirvana is not a positive goal to be achieved in the usual way with years of hard work. It may take years of hard work, but it's not work done to acquire anything; instead, it's practicing letting go of thoughts, an extinction. In theory, and the Buddha says this, it doesn't take any time. How could letting go take more than a moment? Since you already are what you are, realizing it cannot require more than a moment.

The Buddha further describes sages by stating that they live (meaning in thought, speech, and behavior) in accordance with three general resolutions, namely, to avoid doing evil, to do good, and to actualize goodness for others. In other words, they lead lives of selfless service. It's not that they are attached to doing good for others. It's that they understand their actions as naturally benefitting self and other, as if their self concepts include others.

This is why awakening from the addiction to thoughts is the same as morality. Sages have no desire to use others for their own selfish purposes. Why not? They have dissolved attachment to their self-concepts. When they act, they act as if actualizing goodness for others is the same as actualizing goodness for themselves. This explains why they are the only masters of loving.

Sages also live, according to the Buddha, by following ten everyday precepts. To state them dogmatically: cherish life, do not kill; be giving, do not steal; honor the body, do not misuse sexuality; manifest truth, do not lie; keep the mind clear, do not cloud the mind; be understanding and sympathetic, do not speak of other's faults; realize self and other as one, do not elevate oneself and disparage others; give generously, do not withhold spiritual or material aid; actualize harmony, do not indulge in anger; cherish and upload the three treasures, do not revile the three treasures.

These resolutions and precepts are descriptive, not prescriptive. Frankly, it is impossible really to understand any of them without being oneself a sage.

Since a sage lives free from compulsive thoughts, including attachment to self concept, a sage is really a nobody. He or she lives "without-thinking", in other words, in the domain of no-thought rather than thought. This is a self that is no self.

In a sense, then, while it's ordinarily correct to think of a master lover as someone who is incessantly giving to others by promoting what is good for them, that's not really the idea here. That's an outsider's interpretation. The insider's interpretation is that a sage fails to take others to be other at all.

A sage sits in a park or a coffee shop and we think that he or she is watching other people. Actually, he or she is watching other versions of himself or herself. Now there's an interesting idea.

All the words about the three treasures, the four truths for sages, the general resolutions, and the ten precepts are mere stepping stones to help get us to the edge of the conceptual cliff. The point is to let go of land, let go of all thoughts, and be free of all words, concepts, and thoughts. That's what is required to become a sage and to master the art of authentic loving.

As Master Hakuin puts it in his well-known chant: "when we turn inward and prove our True-nature – that True-self is no-self, our own Self is no-self – we go beyond ego and past clever words." A sage is not a separate self somehow loving and becoming one with other separate selves; a sage identifies with other selves and realizes that there is no separation to overcome. The proof requires letting go of concepts and thoughts to realize, as the sage Sengcan put it, that "The One Way knows no differences." The way to realize it is simply to "Cut off all useless thoughts and words."

That realization is required for authentic loving.

8: Preparing for Love

Only sages master the art of loving. Only sages practice authentic love. Only sages are capable of loving without even a trace of selfishness or expectancy or wanting something in return. Only sages are genuinely giving.

Sages speak different languages. They have different theories, different conceptual frameworks. Sages interpret ultimate reality differently.

They do not, however, actually love differently. They identify the divinity in themselves with the divinity in others. They take others essentially to be no better or worse than themselves. In fact, fundamentally, they identify themselves with others.

The process of expanding one's self concept is a natural one. We are not born with self concepts. We learn them. We learn about ourselves from other people who care for us. For example, if they pay attention to us and attend to our needs and desires, we absorb the notion that we are valuable. If they pay as little attention to us as possible and neglect us, we absorb the notion that it's false that we are valuable.

It's normal to learn to identify with one's body. We naturally experience feelings, perceptions, mental formations, and awareness. We begin to make choices based on what we like and what we don't like.

Soon we identify with our caregivers, usually with mother and father. Later we identify with siblings and other relatives and frequent companions. Later we identify with our classmates and members of sports teams we play on or with others who enjoy doing what we enjoy doing such as playing musical instruments or reading or playing games. We come to identify with our geographical local: town, city, state, country. We may even begin thinking of ourselves as earthlings or citizens of the universe.

Love and Respect

We may identify with other kinds of animals, especially sentient ones that make good pets such as dogs. We may even come to identify with lakes or mountains and react passionately when others try to diminish or destroy them.

Sages dissolve barriers between their self concepts and everything else. A fully enlightened sage identifies with everything. That's one way of understanding what happens when the process of preparing for love has been completed. A sage's self concept has expanded to the point where it normally ceases to function as a concept.

Another way of understanding what happens when the process of preparing for love has been completed is to understand it as letting go of attachment to one's self concept. It's not that there is no longer any kind of self concept; it's that it has ceased to function in terms of what is important or valued.

As previously noted, this "process" occurs in a single moment. It may be prepared for for a long time, but it happens in the present moment. After all, it must. It is impossible to live yesterday today, and it is impossible to live tomorrow today. Life occurs in the present moment. Becoming a sage, then, if it is to occur at all must occur in the present moment.

Perhaps it may fruitfully be compared to making a hole in one in golf. It's logically possible for a beginner, on his or her first swing ever of a golf club, to make a hole in one. On the other hand, some players play golf regularly for decades and never make a hole in one. If you learn to play golf properly, the more you play, the more likely it is that you will achieve a hole in one. It could happen at any time or it may never happen.

How, though, does one learn how to let go of all concepts without actually doing it? The task itself is simple: just let go of all thoughts. However, it's very difficult to do that. The Buddha wasn't lying.

Still, it's doing it that counts in terms of loving. Either you will detach from your self concept or you will never master the art of loving. If you really want to love well, then you will do what is required. If you don't, you won't.

Suppose that you do. What should you actually do?

I don't know. Nobody knows! I've explained why that is the case above. It's not just that I am not myself a sage, it's that, even if I were, I would still be incapable of telling you how to awaken from compulsive thoughts. To tell is already to conceptualize. To understand what someone tells you is already to conceptualize.

What is it like?

Usually we tell people what something is like by pointing out appropriate analogies, which means noticing relevant similarities and differences. How, though, could conceptual analogies render what is nonconceptual intelligible to the mind? That's impossible.

If you have never before detached from your self concept, how could you do it? How could you somehow practice or train yourself to do it?

The most popular sage in North America is Jesus. Misunderstandings of his teachings abound. Permit me to single out a couple of his teachings that are relevant here. If we are to believe Luke, Jesus tells us to love all others including our enemies "without expecting any return" [The New English Bible, Luke 6:35.]. Loving others isn't using them to gain something for yourself; it's giving to them what is best for them without even expecting anything in return.

The key to doing that is to drop attachment to your self concept: "'If anyone wishes to be a follower of mine, he must leave self behind . . . What will a man gain by winning the whole world, at the cost of his true self?" [Luke 6: 23 & 25; cf. Matthew 16: 24 & 26.] You can, if you want, spend your whole life gaining and gaining and gaining; however, even if you gain the whole world, you'll have failed to live the best kind of life. You'll have failed to realize your true Self.

To become a sage, as Jesus talks, is to enter the kingdom of God. This is available right here right now: "the kingdom of God is among you" [Luke 17: 21.]. How does he describe it? Very poorly. How could his analogies be very good? He actually asks, "'What is the kingdom of God like?'" [Luke 13: 18-21]. He compares it to a mustard seed that a man plants in his garden that grows to be a tree where birds roost. He compares it to yeast which a woman mixes up with flour until it was leavened. In other words, however living and expansive, it's not so easy to understand. Of course it isn't! Nor is it clear what to do: "By standing firm you will win true life for yourselves." [Luke 21:19.] Yes, but standing firm and not being misled doing what? Maintaining focus, keeping the mind set on the kingdom of God [Luke 12:31]. What, exactly, does that mean? What should we actually be doing? Yes, we should be loving others as ourselves, but how is that possible without detaching from our self concepts?

It's not.

Therefore, the best way to proceed seems to be to be to foster no-thought, nonconceptual awareness. Insofar as we are successful, we'll detach from concepts and, so, from thoughts or judgments. We'll detach from our self concepts.

This is exactly what every kind of body practice is about. We always control our focus, what we think about. If we will train ourselves to focus on something that is always available such as breathing or the aliveness of our bodies, we practice letting go of thoughts. The more we practice letting go of thoughts, the more we are training (purifying, disciplining, stilling, emptying) the mind. The more we do that, the less inclined we are to take things personally. The less inclined we are to take things personally, the more loving we naturally become.

In other words, it's a process of ego attrition. It's logically possible to drop ego delusion the first moment you try, but that's as improbable as making a hole in one the first time you swing a golf club. As you practice golf, the odds of making a hole in one, which could happen on any stroke, shift in your favor. Don't worry about making a hole in one; instead, just focus on becoming a better golfer. You may become a very good golfer without ever making a hole in one. If you make a hole in one, terrific! If not, so?

Similarly, you may become a much better lover even if you never become a sage. You could, at any moment, have a breakthrough. However, as you practice detaching from thoughts, the odds of dropping them completely, which could happen any moment, shift in your favor. Don't worry about becoming a sage, a great lover; instead, just focus on becoming less enslaved by thoughts. You may become a very good lover without ever becoming a sage. If you become a sage, terrific! If not, so?

So, what should be done? I accept the Buddha's answer: meditate.

There are lots of different ways to meditate. Any kind of body practice will do. For example, in chapter 8 of Emotional Eating, I describe how to do aliveness awareness – even when you are watching television. In multiple writings, I have described how to do one kind of meditation, namely, zen meditation, which happens to be the kind that I've been practicing for over 20 years. Permit me to describe it again here.

If you already have a suitable meditation or body practice, you don't need any help from me about it. Please skip ahead to the section "THE CHIEF DANGER OF MEDITATION."

The idea of formal, seated zen meditation is that stilling the body helps in stilling the mind. The still point is when all thoughts are dropped. It's that simple.

It's very easy to learn how to do seated zen meditation. I suggest that western adults begin by using the kneeling posture, which is easier than any of the classic cross-legged postures. I have a short video online in which I demonstrate one classic way to still the body; if you have access to the internet, just go to:
http://www.lasting-weight-loss.com/meditation.html

The body/mind is a whole. The idea is to enable it to quiet down. By stilling yourself physically and mentally, noisy thoughts settle into silence. Distractions settle down.

Let silence reign. Think of compulsive thoughts as like noise. A good way to torture someone is to subject that person to incessant noise. That's what we are unintentionally doing to ourselves; we are subjecting ourselves to incessant noise in the form of compulsive thoughts. All we need to do to live better is to stop doing that.

EQUIPMENT: Here's what you'll need to begin: a quiet place, a blanket, an audible timer, and something suitable to sit on. Permit me to say a bit more about each of these.

A room with a level floor works well. It certainly avoids the problems of sitting outdoors (such as rain, snow, wind, cold, heat, sunlight, darkness, insects or other animals, an unlevel surface, and distracting humans who may pass by). Many rooms are quiet first thing in the morning or late at night even if they are not quiet at other times. Dim light is best. A cool but comfortable temperature is best.

It's possible to buy a special meditation mat, but it's not necessary. Take a large ordinary blanket and fold it into about a 30" square. Put it on the floor with one of its edges a foot or so away from a wall. Even if you don't have the luxury of a carpeted floor, this may provide sufficient cushioning for your knees.

It's possible to buy special meditation timers, but buying one is not necessary. You probably have an audible timer already in your kitchen. Wind it up, set it, and put it far enough away from you so that you cannot hear it ticking but so that you will be able to hear it when it goes off. Alternatively, you may use a timer on your watch or cell phone.

You will need *something to support your hips higher than your knees*. Special meditation cushions or benches are readily available online. If you have some wood, tools, and know how, you may be able to make a bench rather easily. Otherwise, find something that will work such as a rolled-up and folded-over piece of carpet.

STILLING PHYSICALLY: Here are some of the main points. Put your knees on the mat near the edge of the mat that is closest to the wall. Your lower legs should be parallel. Sit back on the support so that your weight is supported by your knees and buttocks. Your hips must be higher than your knees. Push your belly out to tip your hips slightly forward to straighten your spine. Tuck your chin in as if there were a string going from the back of your head to the ceiling.

Pull your shoulders back with your chest up as if there were a string going from your breastbone to the ceiling. Do not lean forward or backward; the back of your shoulders should be above the back of your buttocks. Do not lean to the left or right. Relax your arms completely. Turn your palms up with your dominant hand underneath your other hand. Touch the inner edges of your hands to your lower abdomen. Let the tips of your thumbs touch together lightly at the top of a circle with the forefinger of your nondominant hand as the lower half of the circle.

Keep your mouth lightly closed; do not clench your teeth together. Touch the tip of your tongue just above the inner surface of your top teeth. Lower your eyes so that they are gazing about a foot or so up from the bottom of the wall in front of you.

Take a deep chest breath or two and relax everything except your spine, which should remain erect. (If you later find yourself slumping, sit back up straight.) Breathe with your stomach.

That's it. There should be no strain and your posture should be very stable.

If you sit like that for a while every day, you'll soon become comfortable sitting in that position and be able to do it for 10 or 20 or 30 minutes without discomfort.

Pay attention to any feedback your body gives you. For example, if you notice any soreness the following day in your neck or back, realize that your position was incorrect and make the necessary adjustment. For example, if you feel drowsy during meditation, open your eyes more to let in more light.

If you want another alternative, you may substitute any of the classic cross-legged postures, but none are ever necessary. Nearly everyone finds the kneeling posture easy.

STILLING MENTALLY: The main idea is easy to understand. Just pick something to focus on. Since whatever you focus on grows in importance, as you focus on it more intensely everything else will recede in importance. When you notice that thoughts have arisen, just return to your focus point. Eventually the rate at which thoughts distract you will begin to slow.

Breathing is the classic focal point. You may simply follow the breath in and out. Alternatively, you may count your inhalations and exhalations or just your exhalations. Count silently 1 to 10; when you get to 10, begin again at 1. If you get lost in thought, just begin again at 1.

Eventually, both the thought-object and the thinking subject will vanish together. Sengcan, the third patriarch of Chan [Zen] in ancient China, wrote: "If all thought-objects disappear, / the thinking subject drops away.//For things are things because of mind, / as mind is mind because of things."

Please do not attempt to stop extraneous thoughts from arising. *When thoughts arise, as soon as you notice them return to your focal point.*

Some people are not ready psychologically to meditate. If you experience a panic-attack or other serious problem while meditating, just stop meditating and get some professional help to deal with whatever underlying issue is blocking you. You may resume meditation after that.

THE CHIEF DANGER OF MEDITATION: The chief danger of meditation is inherent in the fact that it is a structured or formal practice. Beginning meditators will notice that there is a gap between how they live during meditation and how they live at other times. For example, if you begin a meditation practice using the instructions provided in the previous section, when you are meditating you will be constantly focused on your breathing whereas at all other times you will not likely be so focused at all. The result is that, even if the mind settles down when you are meditating, it is as likely at other times to be as active as those of non-meditators. In other words, since you are not meditating most of the time, meditation may not do you any good most of the time.

Meditation can become just another routine task like exercising or going grocery shopping. It can become just another item on one's to-do list.

Meditation is a skill. Like all skills, proper practicing enables improvement. People can become excellent at meditating and still have their meditation practice seem irrelevant to the rest of life. They can get very good at progressing through various states of consciousness without ever dropping all thoughts. (This is why, for example, Eckhart Tolle has said that he doesn't teach meditation: he doesn't want what he teaches to be irrelevant to the rest of life.)

This is a real danger. However, it has a genuine solution.

The solution is to extend the focusing to other activities even while leaving formal structured practice sessions behind. Simply keep awareness of breathing with you as much as possible during your ordinary activities. For example, when you are walking down a hallway or putting on a shoe or washing the dishes, there's nothing at all preventing you from focusing on breathing as you move or work. Refuse to separate from practicing.

In fact, the more frequently you can do this throughout the day, the less thoughts will obstruct you.

You may already be familiar with this when physical actions are well-rehearsed such as repeatedly playing a particular piece of music on a piano or serving a tennis ball. When you get wholly into such tasks, you enter the zone. What zone? The zone of no-thought. It's the space where there is no time consciousness or effort or self-consciousness or slavery of any kind. It's the zone of natural freedom from compulsive thoughts (as opposed, say, to different kinds of freedom such as political freedom or freedom of the press). It's what happens when we practice well enough so that we are freed from trying to do something; instead of being stuck trying, we actually become whatever we are doing. Instead of trying to serve the tennis ball, you may just become the serving of the tennis ball. Instead of trying to play the piece of music, you may just become the playing of the music.

In fact, master athletes only ever infrequently think about what they are doing. In competition, there's no time to think. Thinking is too slow, too obstructive.

When you are with others, if you are thinking about loving them, you are almost certainly not loving them well. You may be getting what you are doing correct, but you are not getting how you are doing it correct unless the mind is empty of useless thoughts. If you learn to drop thinking about right and wrong as well as drop trying to gain anything for yourself, you are on the right track. The more that you understand them, the more you will naturally identify with them. The more that you understand what is really good for them, the more you will just automatically promote it.

That's the way that sages, master lovers, love.

This is a simple, radical teaching that has been around for many, many centuries.

Thich Nhat Hanh: "To have a deep and direct understanding of another person, you must become one with him or her. As long as you see yourself as separate from the object, your understanding is not yet true." True understanding requires identification, which automatically results in loving.

The identification comes from emptying the mind of all thoughts and, so, all separation. Sengcan: "Thought cannot reach this state of truth . . . In this true world of Emptiness, / both self and other are no more."

This explains Paracelsus's claim that "he who understands also loves."

9. Communicating Love and Respect

If we are not yet masters of loving, what can we do in addition to continuing the hard work of ego attrition?

Find sages and emulate doing what they do.

For example, Jesus said, "No servant can be the slave of two masters . . . You cannot serve God and Money." [Matthew 6: 24.] It is incoherent to spend part of your time gaining money or other worldly powers or possessions and another part of your time meditating in an effort to drop all attachments to money or other worldly powers or possessions. Trying to compartmentalize life doesn't work well.

For example, Jesus said, "Always treat others as you would like them to treat you" [Matthew 7: 12.] and "Love your neighbor as yourself" [Matthew 22: 39]. Loving yourself more would be violating the 7th Buddhist precept by elevating yourself and disparaging others instead of realizing self and other as one. Jesus recommends loving one another [John 15: 12] and that includes even loving one's enemies [Luke 6: 35.].

For example, Jesus recommends becoming humble like children [Matthew 18:4]. We adults are often far too attached to what we have gained as well as to our thoughts.

A really helpful practice when loving another isn't easy is to tell yourself that that other is really a disguised sage attempting to teach you a lesson for your own good. Suppose, to take a simple example, that someone pulls out in front of you in traffic so that you have to brake your vehicle. You flash anger even though you tell yourself someone else was just being selfish and inconsiderate. You understand that that driver wasn't deliberately targeting you. Maybe it was a physician or surgeon speeding away to save someone's life and you should get out of the way! What's the big deal about getting where you are going more efficiently anyway? As I argue in Getting Things Done, your primary purpose while driving or doing anything else is to be fully engaged in that activity (as opposed to separated from it in thought by being focused on achieving some future good).

All our problems, all human madness, all human suffering, comes from living in slavery to the mind that is dominated by separation. By incessantly thinking and, so, separating mind from body as well as present from past and future, we are living in forgetfulness about the present moment and creating dissatisfaction.

This poisons relationships. Instead of meeting others directly, we take them to exemplify our concepts. Since most of them are doing the same to us, we are never really meeting other people: we remain stuck on thoughts. This explains why loneliness is so pervasive.

The greatest people skill is *not taking things personally*. Sages never take anything personally. Why? Nothing is personal! If someone pulls out in front of you in traffic, that's not about you – it's about that other person. If someone criticizes you, that criticism reveals more about the critic than it will about you. If your lover dumps you, that may mean nothing at all about you but may reveal a lot about your former lover.

Deep listening is a wonderful manifestation of not taking things personally. When you listen to someone, do your best to set aside your preconceptions and pay attention. He or she isn't talking about you. As you listen, stop evaluating. **Gratuitous evaluations poison life**. Start and end with unqualified positive regard. Isn't that how you want others to listen to you?

It's critical to realize that another's surreality is different from your own. You are coming to experiences from different angles. Knowing that is very helpful in not taking things personally. Here are three concrete ways that you may be able to be more loving by applying this general insight.

First, realize that different people learn differently. As soon as you understand this, you'll realize that it explains a lot. Not really understanding others, we often take them to be more like ourselves than they really are. Yes, the divinity that is their core is the same as the divinity that is our core, but their conceptual frameworks as well as their learning styles may be quite different.

Suppose that you are trying to help a loved one understand something. You may assume, incorrectly, that that person learns the same way that you do. If so, your teaching will certainly be inefficient and may be ineffective.

Oversimplifying, there seem to be four different learning styles according to David A. Kolb (via Wyatt Woodsmall and Eben Pagan). We all probably have a degree of each style, but we usually have one style that predominates. For more effective communication, before trying to teach something to a friend, determine your friend's learning style and adjust *how* you teach what you teach. No one style is better than the others. Just understanding that your friend's learning style may not happen to match your own may make a big difference.

Someone who has a predominantly "Why?" learning style always asks, "Why should I learn this?" People with a "Why?" learning style are conceptually blocked from learning something until they understand its importance and, so, have motivation to learn it.

Someone who has a predominantly "What?" learning style always asks, "What am I learning?" People with a "What?" learning style (like me) are conceptually blocked from learning until they understand the context of what they are learning. Without it, they are conceptually disoriented.

Someone who has a predominantly "How to" learning style always asks, "What are the action steps and exercises required?" People with a "How to" learning style are conceptually blocked from learning until they are able to find a correct procedure, recipe, or set of step-by-step instructions that will enable them to learn. Once they have that, then the "why?" and the "what?" will naturally fall into place.

Someone who has a predominantly "What if" learning style always asks, "How can I implement this immediately?" They are action learners. They want to take what they are learning and immediately apply it. They learn best by implementing, getting feedback on the implementation, and then adjusting.

Second, realize that different people have different approaches to reality, different personality types. Your persona is not the same as your personality. A persona is a mask that you wear when dealing with other people; if you want to change it, you may. Your personality is a set of dispositional qualities that are much more fixed. Some psychologists think that they are hard-wired, that we are born with a certain type of personality. They are extremely difficult, perhaps impossible, to change.

Do you have a system for helping you to recognize personality types so that you may communicate with others as effectively and efficiently as possible? If not, permit me to recommend a good one that is effective and neither too simplistic nor too complicated for everyday use. Carl Jung was influenced by ancient Hindu thinkers and this system, the Myers-Briggs Type Indicator (MBTI), was developed from Jung's ideas. It's based on 4 dimensions that come in varying degrees. So, there are 16 personality types. No one type is inherently better than any other type. Each type has inherent strengths and weaknesses.

Furthermore, an individual person may, if each dimension is like a scale, heavily tip the scale in one direction or just barely tip the scale in that direction. In that sense, it allows for endless variety. Nevertheless, it can be very helpful just to focus on the 4 dimensions. Let's use you as an example.

Are you energized more by being with other people rather than being alone and do you like to direct your energy towards others rather than yourself? If so, you are an "extrovert." If not, you are an "introvert."

Do you naturally focus on what is in the present moment (the trees) rather than on the larger picture (the forest)? If so, you are a "sensor." If not, you are an "intuitive."

Do you make decisions logically, objectively, and analytically by weighing the pros and cons rather than relying on how you feel the consequences will affect you and others? If so, you are a "thinker." If not, you are a "feeler."

Do your organize your surreality in a settle, closed way way instead of leaving things in an unsettled, open way? If so, you are a "perceiver." If not, you are a "judger."

The most useful book I have found on using this system is Paul D. Tieger and Barbara Barron-Tieger's The Art of Speedreading People. It may be that the MBTI system is not the best available. My recommendation is only to find and use some such system. If you do, you will become a better lover (whether you are a sage or not yet a sage).

As I wrote in Mastery in 7 Steps: "The sine qua non of good people skills is to forget yourself and focus on the other." It may be interesting to classify yourself using the MBTI, but doing so is not the point here. The point is to use it to classify others. That will enable you to communicate with others by using the language that they naturally speak, which will enable you to establish rapport more easily and quickly with fewer missteps.

I think of it as a bit like wearing clothes. As long as you are dressed in clean, comfortable clothes, it makes very little difference to you how you are dressed. On the other hand, how you are dressed often has a significant impact on others. If, for example, you are married, I recommend dressing to please your spouse.

Similarly, the way that you make a point to someone else makes very little difference to you. On the other hand, how you make it often has a significant impact on others. If, for example, you are married, I recommend speaking your spouse's natural language. If you learn to talk in terms of his or her surreality rather than your own, you will be able to love that person more efficiently and effectively.

Third, a specific instance of this is to realize that different people have different love languages and to learn to speak the love language of your partner. Especially if you are living with someone, why not learn to speak the love language of your partner? It's easy to learn and you will be able to love that person more efficiently and effectively.

Although there are many dialects, Gary Chapman argues in <u>The Five Love Languages</u>, there are five basic love languages. If a husband and wife happen to speak the same love language, that's fine. However, that's not the usual case. If they don't, they may be miscommunicating with each other without realizing it.

Chapman correctly suggests that the "falling in love" experience is not love at all. It fails to meet the minimal criteria for loving. It has nothing to do with deciding anything. It requires no effort, much less sustained effort. It has nothing to do with promoting what is good for the other person. If two people fall in love, at best what they have is a utility sex affair. There's no authentic love without disciplined promoting of what's good for the beloved. The more tainted it is with selfish gaining, the less like authentic love it is.

The different love languages are appropriate for those who are married. They involve using "words that build up," in other words, words that demonstrate appreciation for the beloved, giving the beloved one's full attention, giving gifts that symbolize loving, giving acts of service, and physically touching the beloved in emotionally satisfying ways.

Some of these are appropriate in other loving relationships such as parent/child or teacher/student, but some aren't.

There's no reason to think that these are the only love languages. They may, though, be the ones most appropriate for those who are married.

There are other related topics that relate to loving. For example, there has been a lot of interest recently about differences between male brains and female brains. However interesting, such topics relate to filling out the conceptual framework with respect to loving rather than building it. Both males and females are equally capable of awakening from thought addiction and, so, both are equally capable of authentic loving.

Furthermore, these other topics unfortunately can become mere distractions from the essential and difficult work of ego attrition. **No ego attrition, no authentic love.**

In the previous chapter I indicated how to go about doing that critical work. In this chapter, I indicated how to improve as lovers even before that critical work is finished.

Let's conclude this work on understanding and practicing authentic love.

10: Conclusion

It's appropriate to end a book about authentic loving by reminding ourselves of what some sages have said. St. Francis of Assisi gets it right in his famous prayer.

Sow love when there is hatred. Sow pardon when there is injury. Sow faith when there is doubt. Sow hope when there is despair. Sow light when there is darkness. Sow joy when there is sadness. Seek to console rather than be consoled. Seek to understand rather than to be understood. Seek to love rather than to be loved.

This shift from being self-centered to being other-centered occurs naturally when there is identification with the other, when separation from the formerly other dissolves.

Authentic loving is a natural by-product of the shift from thought to no-thought, of detachment from the self concept. So, instead of becoming distracted by trying to become a better lover directly, focus on making that transition and you will indirectly become a better lover. Sages make that transition. The rest of us fail.

The Buddha recognizes that "It is good to have friends when friendship is mutual," but, still, "If a man who enjoys a lesser happiness beholds a greater one, let him leave aside the lesser to gain the greater." [Quotations here are from The Dhammapada, Easwaran, tr.] Drop attachments to having friends and lovers and, instead, focus on the only non-egocentric desire, the desire to become free of attachment to the ego. This is worth doing and, "If anything is worth doing, do it with all your heart."

"Sitting alone, sleeping alone, going about alone, vanquish the ego by yourself alone. Abiding joy will be yours when all selfish desires end."

Selected Bibliography

Abram, David. The Spell of the Sensuous.

Aristotle. The Complete Works of Aristotle. J. Barnes, ed.

Borg, Marcus, & Riegert, Ray. Jesus and Buddha.

Bradford, Dennis. Compulsive Overeating Help.

Bradford, Dennis. Getting Things Done.

Bradford, Dennis. It's Not Just About the Money!

Bradford, Dennis. Mastery in 7 Steps.

Bradley, F. H. Appearance and Reality.

Buddha, The. Basic Teachings of the Buddha. Glenn
     Wallis, ed.

Buddha, The. The Dhammapada. E. Easwaran, tr.

Buddha, The. In the Buddha's Words. Bhikkhu Bodhi, ed.

Buddha, The. The Connected Discourses of the Buddha.
     Bhikku Bodhi, ed.

Buddha, The. The Long Discourses of the Buddha. Bhikku
     Bodhi, ed.

Buddha, The. The Middle Length Discourses of the
     Buddha. Bhikkhu Bodhi, ed.

Butchvarov, Panayot. Being Qua Being.

Butchvarov, Panayot. Skepticism About the External
     World.

Butchvarov, Panayot. Skepticism in Ethics.

Butchvarov, Panayot. The Concept of Knowledge.

Chapman, Gary. The Five Love Languages.

Cicero. Laelius: On Friendship. Michael Grant, tr.

Edelglass, William, & Garfield, Jay. L., eds. Buddhist
     Thought.

Fisher, Bruce. Rebuilding When Your Relationship Ends.

Fromm, Erich. The Art of Loving.

Hanh, Thich Nhat. Teachings on Love .

Hazo, Robert G. The Idea of Love.

Herrigel, Eugen. Zen in the Art of Archery. R. F. C. Hull, tr.

Kapleau, Philip. The Three Pillars of Zen.

Lao-Tzu. TAOTECHING. Red Pine, tr.

Norretranders, Tor. The User Illusion. J. Sydenham, tr.

Oech, Roger von. A Whack on the Side of the Head.

Plato. The Collected Dialogues of Plato. Hamilton, E., &
    Cairns, H., eds.

Peters, F. E. Greek Philosophical Terms.

Schucman, Helen. A Course in Miracles.

Singer, Irving. The Nature of Love . 3 vols. Second edition.

Solomon, Robert C., and Flores, Fernando. Building Trust.

Stevenson, L., and Haberman, D L. Ten Theories of Human
    Nature. 3rd edition.

Suzuki, Shunryu. Zen Mind, Beginner's Mind.

Tieger, Paul D., & Barron-Tieger, Barbara. The Art of
    Speedreading People.

Tolle, Eckhart. A New Earth.

Tolle, Eckhart. The Power of Now.

Various authors. "Chants & Recitations." Rochester Zen
    Center.

Various authors. The New English Bible. 2ND ed.

Williams, Paul, with Tribe, Anthony. Buddhist Thought .

Williams, Paul. Mahayana Buddhism. 2nd ed.

About the Author

I was born 3 July 1946 in Teaneck, New Jersey, U.S.A. I graduated from Blair Adacemy in 1964. I was a pre-professional philosophy major at Syracuse University and graduated in 1968. After two years as an Army lieutenant with overseas duty in Korea from 1969-1971, I attended graduate school at The University of Iowa where I received an M.A. (1974) and Ph.D. (1977). Panayot Butchvarov was my dissertation director.

I taught humanities and philosophy at SUNY Geneseo from 1977 to 2009. I've written over twenty books; some are listed near the beginning of this book. I founded the Ironox Works, Inc., publishing company in 2004. (If you are interested in finding out about getting your own book done, visit http://ironoxworks.com .)

I'm a former member of MENSA and the American Philosophical Association. I played hockey for many years in the Rochester Metro Hockey League. I've been a member of the Rochester Zen Center for over twenty years. I live happily alone on the shore of Conesus Lake, which is the westernmost of the Finger Lakes in upstate New York.

For more about me, visit the Amazon Author Central page at http://www.amazon.com/-/e/B0047EI11A

If you'd like to connect with me on social media, just go to: http://www.linkedin.com/pub/dennis-e-bradford/1a/a2a/524/ You'll also find there how easy it is to contact me should you wish to do so. And/or http://www.facebook.com/dennis.bradford.313 as well as http://www.twitter.com/dennisebradford

I encourage you to visit my blog on wisdom and well-being: http://dennis-bradford.com . Its posts are grouped in terms of six kinds of well-being (in no particular order) on the sidebar, namely, financial, moral (inter-personal), intellectual, physical, emotional, and spiritual. I encourage you to begin with whatever interests you most. Please feel free to leave comments. I happen to think that there's an enormous amount of free, valuable content there.

Best 3 Suggestions for Additional Reading

Fromm, Erich. <u>The Art of Loving</u>.

Tolle, Eckhart. <u>A New Earth</u>.

Bradford, Dennis. <u>Getting Things Done</u>.

I have a **favor** to ask: If you just finished reading this book, will you please go to amazon.com, locate its description, and leave some feedback? Your review may or may not help me, but it will give others the opportunity to benefit from your judgment. Thank you.

May you love better!

www.ingramcontent.com/pod-product-compliance
Lightning Source LLC
Chambersburg PA
CBHW071836020426
42331CB00007B/1743